Hope And Miracles

A Collection of Poems to Stir Your Emotions

Rashmi Vilas

BookLeaf
Publishing

India | USA | UK

Made with ❤ on the BookLeaf Publishing Platform
www.bookleafpub.in
www.bookleafpub.com

Dedication

To my chirpy daughters Aditi and Amiti, who always inspire and encourage me. My soulmate Vilas, who is the most supportive husband and my best friend for life. Together, we always emerge as winners!

Preface

This book of poems was my dream since years. Although I consider myself as an amateur writer, but I never gave up on my desire to be one. My hopefulness could not fade away with time. My life had many twists and turns, sometimes an emotional rollercoaster.

Being a resilient person, I always learnt to bounce back from the adversities and challenges that life would throw towards me.

This collection of poems will surely imbibe some strong feelings of ambitions, expectations, desires and an overwhelming urge to achieve your dream. Simply inviting miracles in your lives with a soulful gratitude.

Acknowledgements

I would like to thank so many people and some wonderful friends whom I met along the way at various stages. These people not only gave me experiences but also shaped me into a better person. My sincere thanks to my spiritual gurus who guided me in the recent years during the course of spiritual journey. This not only decluttered my thoughts, brought clarity and created a strong impact in my life.

My heartfelt gratitude to my family who were always by my side in all my endeavors. Acceptance of my spiritual learnings with a open mind and also taking baby steps towards the same. They are my pillar of strength and everything in my little world.

1. Expressions of my heart

Delightful joyous expressions on
my face,
Rekindles my pulsing heart to
race,
Determined purposeful promises
to start,
Hopelessness and gloom to fade
apart.

Sparkling eyes that see, beyond
the face,

Throbbing heart that knows, the
silent pace,
In every glance, a mystery is
revealed,
Love's understanding is forever
sealed.

Shoulders strong, a steadfast
stand,
Hands that hold, through life's
uncertain band,
Together bound, through every
test,
Love's support, a guiding light at
its best.

Words are gentle wraps,
embracing hearts in peace,
A listening shore, where
emotions freely release,
Rivers are tears, flowing true and
deep,
A safe haven's refuge, where
love's solace keep.

Expressions of heart, like petals
unfold,
Soft whispers of comfort, like
sparkle of gold,
Listening hearts, like beacons
bright,

Navigating through darkness, to
love's warm light.

2. Laughter

Smiles shared are contagious
glee,
Laughter echoes are loud and
free,
Infectious joy in hearts now
light,
Connections born are pure
delight.

Smiles collide and laughter spills,
Joyful echoes in heart that thrills,

Moments merge and eyes gently
meet,
Connections spark and heart
skips a beat.

Laughter echoes with a joyful
sound,
Sparkling eyes our heads turned
around,
A joyful gaze and love takes a
flight,
Romance sparks a pure blissful
delight.

Love shines bright in laughter's
glow,

Hands entwined, in joy they
grow,
Soft whispers sweet, tender touch
true,
Warm smiles, divine fragrance
shines through.

Laughter's spark, kindles soul's
delight,
Hearts swirled in love's warm,
golden light.
Tender whispers like gentle
morning dew,
Warm smiles and love's radiance,
forever true.

3. Beyond Words

Soft whispers in the dead of
night,
Warm fingers intertwined a
gentle light,
The scent of roses, sweet and
true,
Love's fragrance forever shining
through.

Hands that entwine, hearts that
beat,
Eyes that sparkle, souls that

meet,
In every touch, a promise made,
Love's connection forever
displayed.

In whispers, tears or joyful
sound,
Our emotions paint the truth
around,
In every line there's a story's told,
Of love, loss, dreams and hearts
of gold.

Eyes sparkle bright, in laughter's
glow,
Hearts entwined, in joy they

grow,
Soft candlelight, warm gentle
hue,
Love's masterpiece, each moment
is true.

Softly held hands, in loving care,
Tender moments, beyond
compare,
Gentle love, that soothes the
soul,
Tender affection, makes us
whole.

4. Hope and Aspirations

Hope's soft whisper, calms the
night,
Glittering stars, twinkle with
gentle light.

In darkness, hope's ember glows,
Warming hearts, with promise
that flows.

When shadows fade, hope's light
prevail,
Illuminating paths, through life's

trail.

Dreams take flight, on
aspiration's wings,
Soaring high, where heart's
passion clings.

With every step, our journey's
decide,
Aspirations fuel, the heart's inner
tide.

In pursuit of dreams, our goal
takes a leap,
Aspirations lift our spirit and
vision we keep.

Hope's gentle breeze, fans
aspirations flame,
Navigating us forward through
life's noble game.

With hope's spark, aspirations
take flight,
Enlightening fearless path to
endless height.

Through life's journey, hope's
anchor holds fast,
Aspirations lift our spirit's in this
world so vast.

5. Echoes of Love

Love's echoes are mighty ocean
waves,
Crashing on shores, where
memories crave.

Heartbeats whisper, love's Morse
code,
Echoes resonating forever in
vibrant mode.

Love's fragrance lingers, scent so
sweet,

Echoes of memories forever a
soulful treat.

Echoes are brushstrokes, painting
the past,
Love's a grand masterpiece,
forever to last.

Love's echoes are melodious
musical notes,
Harmonizing hearts in
scintillating tones.

Echoes are footprints, on golden
sands,
Love's journey clasped by tender
hands.

Love's echoes ripple, like moonlit
tides,
Whispers of memories, where
hearts reside.

Heartstrings vibrate, with love's
gentle tone,
Echoes of love resonating,
forever abode.

Love's fragrance spreads, like
morning dew,
Echoes of memories, forever
pristine and new.

6. Illusions Dreams and Reality

Illusions wilt, like frost-kissed blooms,
Reality's chill, winter's darkest glooms.

Dreams evaporate, like morning dew,
Leaving emptiness, in shadows anew.

In illusion's maze, mirrors reflect my past,

Reality's lens, focuses on truth at
last.

Dreams whisper secrets, in
midnight's hush,
But truth's harsh voice, echoes
'awake and rush'.

Illusions are autumn leaves,
rustling free,
Reality's winter, freezes
memories in plea.

Dreams are morning dew,
evaporating fast,
Leaving emptiness, that will
forever last.

Illusions are silk threads, fine and
agile,
Reality's boulders, crush dreams
fragile.

Dreams are moonbeams, dancing
on the floor,
Reality's darkness, snuff lights
and close door.

Dreams manifest peace, diffusing
illusions away,
Reality's sun shines bright,
keeping darkness at bay.

7. Tides of Nostalgia

Hope's compass navigates,
through uncharted tide,
Nostalgia anchors our hearts
where memories reside.

Memories of love, like beacons
shine so bright,
Illuminating paths, to dawn's
warm, golden light.

Dazzling stars of hope, sparkle
like diamonds rare,

Nostalgia is wisdom, whispers
secrets we care.

Heart's memories echo, 'You're
strong, you're true',
Leading us forward, to a brighter
future anew.

Tides of nostalgia, recollect
reminiscences home,
Waves of gratitude, gather
moments in delightful tone.

Nostalgia's whispers,
encompasses our past,
But hope's promise, illuminates

the path at last.

Storms of life subside, like waves
at the shore,
Nostalgia's lessons, teach us to
endure some more.

Moments cherished in nostalgia's
golden dream,
Are footprints on sand of as we
blush and scream.

Shadows of past, like silhouettes
they stare,
Heart's recollections, like pages
valuable and rare.

8. Blissful Echoes

Soft whispers echo, like jasmine
fragrance,
Blissful essence, lingers in
conscience .
Moonbeams dance, on memories
past,
Echoes of bliss, forever should
last.

Heartbeats resonate, there to
inspire.
Blissful echoes, manifest heart's

desire.

Echoes whisper secrets, in silence
deep,

Mystic bliss in remembrance we
keep.

Blissful echoes, linger like
sunset's glow,

Warmth of flashbacks forever to
know.

Echoes of bliss are vibrant
autumn leaves.

Golden reminiscences, forever
we retrieve.

Echoes whisper like cool summer

breeze,
In tender fragments of blissful
time freeze.
Ephemeral glimpses of euphoria
in a leap,
Heart-swelling joy, forever we
reap.

Echoes of bliss, joyful instant of
pure delight,
Warmth and comfort, on a cold
winter night.
Moments of unbridled happiness
never fade,
Manifesting ecstatic joy and
blissful shade.

9. The Weight of Silence

Silence is a canvas, painted with
unseen hues,
A refection of emotions, that
words cannot muse.

The weight of unspoken words,
like stones in the sea,
Sinks deep into the heart, where
embedded secrets be.

Silence is a garden, where each
thought takes root,

Nourished by reflection, where
wisdom is a fruit.

The weight of silence, like wild
showers of rain,
The soul grow stronger, through
life's joys and pain.

Silence whispers truths, in quiet
hushed hours,
A reflection of heart, in calm
sereneness towers.

The weight of unspoken words,
like autumn leaves,
Falls softly, revealing our life's
hidden themes.

Silence is a mirror, reflecting
soul's intricate design,
A canopy for emotions, in
numerous shades divine.

The weight of silence, like
ocean's remotest depths,
Guide us inward, where
profound wisdom dwells.

Silence is a calm river, spanning
deep and wide,
Reverberating unspoken truths,
where secrets reside.

The weight of unspoken words,
like smoke rising high,
Purifies the soul, where the truth
meets the eye.

10. Wings of Hope

Beneath wings of hope, there lies
peace,
A refuge from life's turbulence
release.
With wings outstretched, we face
the test,
And rise above, to obtain some
rest.

Freedom's wings, like a liberation
song,
Echoing hope, where hearts

belong.
Transformed by love we spread
our wings,
And soar anew, with joy that
clings.

With every stroke, our hearts
take flight,
Soaring on winds, of promise and
light.
Dark shadows of fear, fade with
time.
As wings of hope, behold us and
bind.

In darkest night, when fears

unfold.
Wings of hope with love enfold.
Fluttering rapidly, they lift us so
high,
Above all pain, to touch the
morning sky.

With hope's wings guiding, we
find our way,
Through life's darkest nights, to a
brighter day.
Their gentle caressing, calms
anxious mind,
And lead us forward, to a fearless
ride.

11. New Beginnings

Brilliant sunshine, warm and
bright,
Brings new beginnings, filled
with delight.
The world awakens, fresh and
new,
A chance to start , with dreams
anew.

Like flowers blooming, vibrant
and bold,
New possibilities here unfold.

Every step forward, a story's told,
Of hope and joy, each page
unfold.

With a heart full of hope, and
spirit free,
I dance into the day, with
happiness and glee.
Every moment's chance, to start
anew,
To chase my goals and make
dreams true.

The scenic vibrant hues, paint a
beautiful sight,
A magical fresh beginning,

shining with delight.
A chance to rediscover, and make
life worthwhile,
With every breath, I feel so zesty
and thrive.

In every sunrise, a chance to
shine,
To pursue my dreams, and make
them mine.
New beginnings bring, a heartful
of cheer,
A fresh start's promise, a brighter
year.

12. Embers of Passion

Deep within, a glowing hope
remains,
Embers of passion, that refuse to
wane.

A spark within, that flickers
bright,
Guiding me forward through
life's darkest night.

Like autumn leaves that smolder
slow,

The embers of passion, a gentle
glow.

A warmth that spreads, through
heart and soul,
Reminding me, of dreams that
make me whole.

In moments still, I surely feel the
heat,
Embers of passion, that burn so
deep.

A fire that fuels, my deepest
desire,
To chase my dreams, and reach
for higher.

With every breath, the embers
glow,
A light that guides, through life's
ebb and flow.

The warmth of embers, on skin
so fine,
A gentle caress, that soothes me
soul's confine.

A crackle of flames, a symphony
so sweet,
Echoes through my heart, a
rhythm to repeat.

Like a river's current, that flows

strong and free,
The embers of passion carry me
to destiny.

13. Whispers of Longing

The smell of rain, on a summer's
day,
Brings back memories, of love all
the way.

The eyes full of tears, that fall
like rain,
Echoes of longing, that refuse to
wane.

The warmth of sunbeams, on
skin so fair,

Reminds me to love, that's
beyond compare.

The sound of laughter, that giggle
so clear,
A joyful melody, that dispels all
fear.

In moonlit gardens where
shadows play,
The whispers of longing, come
out to sway.

The fragrance of bloom, that fills
the night,
Intoxicates my senses, with
mesmerizing delight.

The warmth of breath, like your
tight hug,
Sends shivers down with a loving
smug.

The taste of honey, that's sweet
as your kiss,
Leaves me longing, for love's
tender bliss.

14. Seeking Magic

In twilight's hush, where
shadows dance,
Magic whispers, secrets, in a
mystic trance.

Like a master chef, who blends
rare spices,
The universe mixes magic, in
subtle devices.

The fragrance of moonflowers,
that bloom at night,

Guides me to hidden paths,
where magic's in site.

The glittering stardust on my lips
so fine,
Leaves a trail of splendor, that's
simply divine.

Like a lotus blooming in radiant
light,
Beauty of magic unfurls, with all
it's might

The scent of blossoms, that linger
in the air,
Invigorates my senses, with a
magic so rare.

In every sunrise, enchanting
magical gleams,
A new beginning unfolds, like
joyful dreams.

With every step ahead, magic's
path unwinds,
A marvelous journey, that heart
and soul entwines.

In nature's beauty, the essence of
magic I find,
A sense of amazement, that's
forever aligned.

15. Journey Inward

In the bottom my soul, a little
lantern of gold,
Illuminating shadows, where
secrets unfold.

A divine fragrance, lingers
through my mind,
As I steer through the maze, the
truth to find.

Like a lotus blossoming, in the
darkness below,

My heart unfurls it's petals,
wisdom begins to grow.

The flavor of self-awareness, like
nectar on my lips,
Sweetens my perception, as inner
truth grips.

In the still dark night, stars
dazzle like diamonds bright,
Reflecting celestial compass, that
guides my inner light.

My heartbeats sound, like drums
pounding in my chest,
Pulsates with a purpose and goal,
as my soul finds rest.

With the soul's journey inward,

the divine path unwinds,

Disclosing hidden treasures, my

heart and soul entwines.

A feeling of inner peace, in cool

breeze as my life spins,

Soothes my soul's longing, as my

inner journey begins.

16. Embracing Self-love

Like a maestro conducting, my
heart's symphony,
Embracing self-love in perfect
harmony.

I orchestrate self-love by
honoring my needs,
Embracing my true self, setting
clear boundaries.

The fragrance of lavender
whispers, calmness in my soul,

As I nurture my spirit, I find
strength for my goal.

The taste of ripe mangoes
sweetens my perceptions,
Self-worth and lovableness are
cherished conceptions.

Like an expert painter, I color my
canvas bright,
With strokes of self-acceptance,
and hues of delight.

Like a river flowing smoothly,
my emotions attune,
As ripples of self-love take my
heart to the moon.

The stars of self-compassion
glitter and shine,
Guiding me through life's
journey, that's divine.

In the silence of self-reflection, I
hear my inner voice,
A whisper of wisdom that makes
my heart rejoice.

The beauty of my flaws, like a
unique piece of art,
Make me more precious,
prepping up for a new start.

17. Winds of Change

The winds of change humming a
melody so clear,
A symphony of hope evolves
dispelling all fear.

Like a butterfly emerges, from a
cocoon so bright,
I spread my wings of freedom to
take a flight.

The sound of leaves rustling, and
the fireflies glow,

Echoes the secrets, that only
change can show.

Like autumn gusts, sweeping the
trees so tall,
The winds of change blow strong
to transform us all.

The crashing sea waves, like a
refreshing ocean kiss,
Invigorates my spirit, towards a
journey of pure bliss.

The winds of change, awaken
like the sun rising high,

Bringing new beginnings, and a
luck to touch the sky.

The winds of change are wings,
that lift me to soar,
Masking the doubts and fears,
that made me close door.

The winds of change, dance with
merry steps in sight,
Bringing joy and smiles, to
banish the darkest night.

They carry the fragrance, of
blossoms so sweet,
Filling my heart with bliss,
dancing to a happy beat.

Like a ship navigating, through
unchartered sea,
I chart my course, where the
winds of change set me free.

18. Power of Faith

Spark of faith ignites a flame,
burning with might,
Warming my heart with hope,
expelling gloomy night.

The tender touch of faith brings
solace to my soul,
Calming fears and doubts,
making my spirit whole.

The power of faith is sunrise
painting the sky with gold,

Warms my heart with hope and
makes my spirit bold.

The fragrance of blossoming
jasmine whirls around me,
As the gentle breeze of faith
whispers melodies to me.

Like a Culinary Maestro, faith
mixes ingredients of trust,
Adding dashes of courage and
spoonsful of love that's just.

Faith's melody whispers
mesmerizing tunes so pure,
A symphony of joyful mood for

my heart to endure.

The rhythm of faith's echoes
through my heart's deep core,
Sings a chorus of assurance that
soothes me even more.

Like a skilled architect, faith
crafts a foundation strong,
A base of firm conviction, where
dreams and hopes belong.

The building of faith stands
resilient through the tide,
A dream world of peace, where
love and hope ride.

19. Divine Guidance

The flavor of divine guidance
enriches each step I take,
A soulful recipe for miracles
unfolds with purpose and grace.
,
Divinity is a celestial navigator,
navigating life's course
Providing guidance and clarity,
charting the trajectory and
source.

The soothing tunes of divine

grace echo through my mind,
A symphony of hope and
promise that forever will
entwine.

A glow of divine lantern lights
up my path so bright,
Illuminating the journey through
life's darkest night.

Divine guidance is a guiding star
navigating life's new roads,
Offering directions and insights
to reach the highest abodes.

Divine inspiration echoes a soft
murmur in my warm heart,

It is a soothing voice of wisdom
that sets me apart.

Divine guidance is a gentle
stream flowing through my soul,
Quenching my thirst for wisdom
and making my heart whole.

Divine guidance is a shelter from
life's turbulent storms,
A haven where I find solace, and
my spirit transforms.

Like a skilled artist, it paints a
masterpiece so fine,
With colors of hope and joy, that

forever will shine.

20. Karmic Connections

Soulmates converge like stars in
a celestial dance,
Their connection is embroidered
in the fabric of chance.

A karmic thread weaves through
the tapestry of fate,
Binding hearts together, in a
bond so great.

The scent of destiny whirls
through the air of compassion,

As their hearts entwine in a truly
divine passion.

Like a fragrant rose, their karmic
connection blooms,
Unfolding petals of trust and
warmth over the moon.

The universe conspires to bring
them to this mystic place,
Where their hearts entwine in a
sacred karmic space.

Their karma is a canvas, painted
with vibrant hues,
A triumph of moments that is
forever infused.

The brushstrokes of fate create a
marvel so fine,
An unbreakable bond and a love
truly divine.

The cosmic love sweetens every
moment shared,
A karmic connection infused
deep and cared.

With every step, they weave a
karmic tale of gold,
A tale of two celestial souls,
forever to unfold.

Karmic connection is a bridge in

time and space,
Leading them to each other, with
a calm, loving pace.

21. Phoenix Rising

Like a phoenix rising, we spread
our wings,
And take our flight, where love
and joy cling.

Like a phoenix rising, from ashes
reborn,
My soul's deepest yearning
comes along.

With every beat, the heart sings
an exciting song,

A melody of hope, where
fragrant love belongs.

In the eye of the storm, it is hard
to find a peaceful place,
A calm within the chaos, where
wisdom takes a space.

The glow of sunrise at dawn, like
a phoenix rising high,
Signals new beginnings, born
from a red fiery sky.

With wings of joy, the phoenix
leaps to the sky,
A burst of colorful feathers, as it
rises high.

The sun shines bright, on its
radiant, glowing face,
Illuminating hope and miracles
in a sacred space.

With every powerful leap, it finds
a perfect way,
Through the surrounding
darkness to a brighter day.

The spirit of the phoenix is a
flame that burns so bright,
Guiding us forward, through the
darkness of night.

The phoenix rising is a symbol of

determination and might,
A strong reminder that we can
rise above the night.

www.ingramcontent.com/pod-product-compliance
Lightning Source LLC
LaVergne TN
LVHW011045200726
843509LV00011B/1352